THE DIARY OF A MODERN POET.

THE DIARY OF A MODERN POET.

my readers,
if this book is in your hands, i hope you find pieces of yourself in it.
my heart has made a home of these pages— and you just might find
that yours has *too*. i wrote this for the lovers, the broken-hearted, and
the fixer-uppers… i wrote this for those who may have lost
themselves for a while— or are still lost. the ones who feel too
deeply— or feel nothing at all. chances are, if this book is in your
hands, you're in the right place.

love always,
M.L. Scorns.

THE DIARY OF A MODERN POET.

to T,
thank you for giving me what i needed to write this.

to B,
thank you for believing in me.

THE DIARY OF A MODERN POET.

contents

chapter 1

the scorning

THE DIARY OF A MODERN POET.

i spent most of my time being
the object of my own scorn.
i'd sit and pick myself apart—
petal by petal; *limb by limb.* if someone had told me a thorn was too
sharp, i'd cut it off with no hesitation. but, these pieces— they always
grew back. and with time, i learned that no amount of trimming
myself would change my roots;
that i'd always grow a certain way and i could never truly love
myself as long as i believed that some parts were just
unworthy.

THE DIARY OF A MODERN POET.

how foolish am i
for letting myself get burned
time and time again

and for loving the arsonist.

'how did i get here again?'
i asked myself, like a frightened child, on the bathroom floor.
remembering what it was like last time
and the time before that;
refusing to look into the mirror because
what if everything they said about me was true?

it felt like it killed you and in a way,
it did.

-reincarnated

just as i began to breathe again,
you held my head underwater.
and this was the moment i realized that as long as i loved you,
i'd suffocate.

i don't really think of you anymore.
but when i do—
i wonder where you are and who you're hurting. i send silent
messages of hope to anyone ill-fated enough to have crossed your
path. i say to them 'it's a long road ahead,
but i survived it
and you will too.'

do not fear being the villain in other people's stories.
sometimes all it takes to be the villain is to
nick them with the knife that they've been using to slice you open
for years.

i have respect for the sinners who *know* they're sinners.
it's the ones that neatly pack their sins in a suitcase and
hide it where no one can see that frighten me.
waving their store bought halos around,
in a way that says
'look! look at me, i'm *good.*'

you preyed on me the way a snake preys on a mouse; you eyed me up for size and swallowed me whole.

-i was just a kid

being deceitful about who you are is a surefire way to break
someone's heart.
it is *cruel*—
to trick someone into falling in love with a person you know doesn't
exist; to let them live in an illusion.

i gave pieces of myself out carelessly;
to anyone who asked.
'here is my love, *here* is my energy, *here*, just take it.'
and i'm not saying that's a *bad* thing. i just needed to learn when to
stop giving because if you let them, they'll rob you of everything you
have—
including yourself.

THE DIARY OF A MODERN POET.

i write about you still.
not because i miss you
nor do i still love you, but because monsters make good stories.
and who's best to tell them
other than the people who have seen them
up close.

i watched her shatter at 3 am; drunk and afraid.
puffy eyes.
speaking of things she's never said aloud before.
'you're still beautiful.' i told her.
maybe even more now
than ever.

he lied the way he *breathed.*
each breath;
each deceit seemed vital;
like he needed them to keep himself alive.

i held my hand out to him for years and
the *exact* moment someone else grabbed it was when he said:
'*wait,* i was almost ready.'

'goodbye' has always had
a hard time slipping from my lips.
the feeling of glass rising from my throat—
sometimes swallowing it back down because it was just
too sharp of a thing to say.

THE DIARY OF A MODERN POET.

i am well aware of the collateral damage that took place
in the war against myself.
i wish *healing* on the wounded;
and i wish *forgiveness* for myself.

THE DIARY OF A MODERN POET.

i once tried to use someone
to forget someone else

and that was the cruelest thing i've ever done.

so much of my life
has disappeared.

it's blurry,
like a movie i wasn't really in
rather than just watching it
drunkenly from the audience.

and when we met, there was a sort of familiarity to him.
an ease;
like we were *very* distant friends.
and when we spoke, i did not have to think of how to form my words;
like we shared a language that no one else ever took the time to
understand.

if i could go back in time, i'd find her and i'd tell her:
leave him.
because i'd give my life if it meant
hers was kinder.

-to the women before me

they will slice you open
then blame you for bleeding.

he poisons you and then asks you why you are so sick.
'get over it.' he says, as he feeds you another teaspoon.

i've come to find that
anger is the easiest emotion to feel;
it is the ego's best friend.

THE DIARY OF A MODERN POET.

you made me feel
like a *burden*
like our relationship was this puzzle
that you really only worked on
when you had nothing else to do
and even then
i knew
that you would choose

a prettier
and an easier one
when it came along.

THE DIARY OF A MODERN POET.

the person that i loved
lied so intensely,
that eventually—
his words began to sound like scripts;
well-written and well-rehearsed.
i'd gaze at him during his dialog and wonder how someone could
play a part so well. and the worst part is, after him,
all i see are actors.

i hope you find what you're looking for
but i fear for it when you do.

be weary of whoever seems *too* much like you.
sometimes predators don't wear masks; they wear mirrors.

when he loved me, he only loved me halfway.
and when he left me, he only left me halfway.
it was as if he did not want my heart but he did not want anyone else
to have it *either*.
how selfish;
to hold onto something simply so no one else can touch it.

THE DIARY OF A MODERN POET.

i used to leave the door open
for when you decided to come back

then i shut it
then i locked it

then i poured gasoline on it
and burned it to the ground.

i won't be here
when the music stops playing
and the bottles run dry.

- this party was always your choice,
not mine.

being betrayed by a lover tells you that someone's _flesh_
was worth more than your heart,
your soul,
your spirit.
i've never known anything to be so cruel—
so shattering.

i made the mistake of revealing *too* much, *too* soon.
i handed him the roadmap to my heart and he followed it perfectly
until he finally got there and began destroying it.
i know better now.
i know to let people show me who they are before i tell them
who i'm looking for.

THE DIARY OF A MODERN POET.

i often feel out of place

like a puzzle piece
in the wrong puzzle
and everyone notices.

loving someone is *terrifying*.
it's like walking blindfolded into the street and
just having to trust that you won't get hit.
even though
most of the time—
you do.

i wish for you to meet yourself
in a lover

i wish for you to feel what i felt
when you were mine

i knew the moment he looked at a stranger
with more love in his eyes
than he ever looked at me,
there was nothing i could ever do to make him *stay*.

you do not get to walk away
then make me feel guilty
or *ashamed*
for what i do
with the space that you chose
to leave behind.

and my mind knows that the past is not worth holding on to.
it says to old memories:
'you don't belong here anymore.'
i only wish that my body did the same.
instead,
it holds each memory like a secret, too ashamed to let go of.

THE DIARY OF A MODERN POET.

and when i ask myself
if i love you

the answer is
i love who you were supposed to be

THE DIARY OF A MODERN POET.

i find myself asking
what could have made you so cruel

for the world has broken me as well

but i could never be like you.

THE DIARY OF A MODERN POET.

you stabbed me,
then put the bandaid on

and for the longest time,
i thought that was *love*.

he will never find love because he doesn't know what it looks like.
he thinks that love is picking a flower from the dirt simply because it
is pretty.
then when he realizes that he's gotten dirt on his hands, he gets
frustrated,
yelling that that's not what he asked for.
then the flower starts to die because it has not been watered
and he gets *furious*.
it's not pretty enough for him anymore.
the petals have wilted.
he thinks to himself that it was just a bad flower, and the next one
will be better,
only for that one to
die *too*.

THE DIARY OF A MODERN POET.

my first drink tasted like the medicine i had been needing for a long time; and *this was the very moment i became sick.*

i am still healing from the hurt others have inflicted upon me; but more importantly, i am still healing from the hurt that i've inflicted upon myself.

-self destruction

THE DIARY OF A MODERN POET.

i ask myself
why do i write so much about love?

the truth is,
i haven't written much about love *at all*.

there are people whom you can love dearly—
but need to stay away from.
people who came from the same kind of dark you come from,
but haven't found their way out.
you might spend your entire life trying to get them to see the light but
in the end,
they'll only rob you of your own.

i wish i had learned sooner that mistakes are just that; *mistakes.*
i spent too long keeping people around who maliciously and
consciously hurt me because i thought that they deserved second,
third, or fourth chances to love me.
looking back, it was *insanity*—
to keep handing the knife back to the people who just wouldn't stop
making me bleed.

i spend most of my time alone because
i've learned that is where i'm safe.
and some might say that's not living—
and maybe it's not. but for right now,
safe feels like a very good thing to be.
for right now, i'm okay with not playing the game of who will burn
me and
who will not.

chapter 2

homesick

people told me what i *should* be and i molded myself into that like a
piece of clay.
scraping the excess parts off—
because they said they were *too much*.

THE DIARY OF A MODERN POET.

i used to despise you for walking away.
but i've come to realize that
maybe, just maybe,
walking away was the only way you knew how to truly love me.

THE DIARY OF A MODERN POET.

if i have learned anything in this lifetime,
it's that **we cannot escape ourselves.**
our vices were only ever rain checks.
i spent saturday night drinking myself away and yet—
i was the first person i ran into on sunday morning.

that place was hauntingly empty.

-the home i create will be different
than the home i came from.

i got so used to playing in the fire that not being burned began to grow boresome.

-my chaos itch

alcohol is a murderer disguised as a *friend*.
and i've grieved too many deaths in this lifetime;
including *my own*.

you'll never regret fighting for love.
even if it ends in shambles, at least you can say
you tried.

do not to compare where you are in life to other people.
you may be running on sand while they're running
on concrete.

do not let people treat you like a pit stop;
a place convenient enough to visit along the way—
but never enough
to stay.

THE DIARY OF A MODERN POET.

healing is one thing;
bandaging our wounds, tending to them as they begin to fade.
repairing is another;
gathering our pieces.

gluing, taping, welding ourselves like a puzzle that we know will
never look quite the same again.

getting my forgiveness is not difficult.
i have always handed out chances as if they were pencils i didn't
mind borrowing.
and i don't know if that makes me a saint—
or a fool.

THE DIARY OF A MODERN POET.

for as long as i can remember
i've been missing something

and i still haven't figured out what it is
or where to find it.

i am shackled to the grief
of who i used to be.

THE DIARY OF A MODERN POET.

i hope you always find your way back to what you love.
whether it be writing, painting, dancing, or a *person*.
i hope you choose to follow your heart in a world that tries to
convince you it's useless.

i adore the rawness of humanity.
i don't want friends who laugh with me over drinks just to go home
with a head still as full of thoughts as it was before they arrived.
i want truth, i want tears, i want to see someone for who they are
underneath it all and i want *them* to see me that way too.
i want connection;
a connection that makes both of us feel lighter.

THE DIARY OF A MODERN POET.

you were my always
and i was your maybe.

a child who was not shown love will grow to be one of two things:
someone who yearns for it
or someone who runs from it

THE DIARY OF A MODERN POET.

a sense of self is something that i lack.
i'm not sure when or where i lost it.
maybe it was the first time i picked up a bottle.
or maybe it was when i loved a man who robbed me of all things
good.
anyway, i'll find me again.
i'm *somewhere*—
here or there; in between these pages.

i held onto you
as if my life depended on it

and at the time,
it felt like it did.

-codependency

but *i stayed.*
i sat there on the sofa like a fool,
watching the same sad film
over and *over*—
hoping for a different ending.

they love what they cannot have;
this is why they don't love you until you begin to love someone else.

i have never had a person that didn't try to come back.
months—
or even years later.
they always say the same thing;
that they didn't know what they had.
that they didn't realize how muggy the air was until they stopped
breathing *mine*.
because of this,
i no longer feel sorry when people leave.
at least,
not for me.

i feel sorry for those who think art is silly
and love is nothing but a transaction;
who let their minds drag them somewhere entirely different than
where their heart wants to be because that's what they were told they
should do.
this is not experiencing life for what it should be.
this is robotic.

i saw a photo of you today.
and what made me so emotional is that—
i didn't recognize you.
i mean,
physically, you've changed, as we all do with age.
but i could see in your eyes that you aren't the person that i loved and
instead, *you're a stranger.*
i think it gave me some closure;
that i don't know who you are anymore so how could i say that i still
love you, right?
i can't love a stranger. but i will say,
whoever you are now,
i hope you're happy.

THE DIARY OF A MODERN POET.

i forgive you
for the things you did

after all,
you were still a kid.

THE DIARY OF A MODERN POET.

he started something in me
that i still haven't quite figured out
how to put out.

make sure you are healing and not just forgetting
because trust me,
you'll remember.

-what you're running from is faster than you

you will search for my laugh in hers
and you'll ache at the moment it's *close enough.*
you will feel for my heart in her chest
and it will be too late by the time you realize—
you don't find
the same heart *twice.*

i've always been the one that they come back for;
like the town that they left because they thought there was some place
better for them.
only to find that it's not as exciting out there as they thought it would
be and they start missing home.
i'll know i've met the love of my life when he never wants to leave
because he knows what he has—
without having to lose it *first*.

and don't forget the way that
you asked them to choose you—
and **they acted like their hands were tied.**

and i have learned to love you from afar—
the way i love my hometown.
i still think of you fondly,
but i know it's not where i belong.

your love visits in the summer—
but runs at the first changing leaf.
it was a cruel way to learn that your love was never
mine to keep.

change is difficult for many;
myself included.
it's surreal—
just as soon as you get used to one world,
you get transported to another with no idea of how to navigate it.

holding onto us felt like holding onto barbed wire
and letting go was the moment i began to heal.

i made a home out of you
and i should've known better
by the way that you made
leaving seem so easy

-evicted

love is not something to ask for; to plead for. if you must first negotiate, then you are not receiving love— you're receiving tolerance.

oh, his rainy days. i'd hold an umbrella in one hand and *his* hand in the other. i'd look at him with love in my eyes that said *'don't worry, i'm not going anywhere.'*

-unrequited love

there is a place for you in my heart;
a small room
filled with books and tea and a fireplace in the corner.
with me,
you'll always have a place
to call home.

i think i'll always miss you;
the way i'd miss my eyesight or sense of smell.
i know i could live without them, i wouldn't *want* to.

-the missing sense

i've been searching for myself for as long as i can remember. and i'm right there, at the tip of my fingers.

your love
was the kind of love
that made it easier to breathe.

i've left the bridge open
for far too long—
hoping that the ones that have departed from me might find their way
back.
but i'm starting to realize, it's not about finding their way back. i
never moved.
maybe it's time i did.

i call you sometimes still, just to say hi;
just to hear your voice.
and you answer, because you still care;
enough to say hi, enough to listen to my voice. and that's all that we
have left of each other.
moments of small talk and of comfortable silence. the 'how are
you's' that really mean:
i still wish it was us in the end.

people say that when we're lost, we aren't meant to find ourselves,
we are meant to *create* ourselves—
and i believe this to be true. but i think there *is* a sliver of ourselves
meant to be found.
maybe a part of us that we lost when we grew up.
a spark, a joy, a root.
there's something that no matter how much you create, you feel you
need to find your way back to.

i'm ready to pack a bag. just one. and i'm ready to leave the rest
behind.
this life that i've been living is not for me; it never was.
this hurt was never mine to hold.
these people were never mine to love.
and this town was never mine to call home.

chapter 3

the color blue

i was 13 the first time blue visited me. and we laid in bed together for weeks. until a relative recognized who i was spending time with— because they were once visited too.

-our genetic friend,
the color blue

i come from a glass home.
one move too sudden—
it'd all come crashing down.
and picking up the pieces was often my job;
cutting up my hands as i tell everyone '*look*, i'm fixing it.'

i searched for myself in other people, in loud bars, and in clouds of smoke. i spent so long looking for myself in the wrong places and all i ever found
was *chaos*.

i've seen my mother wear heartbreak on her face
more times than makeup;
and i've befriended the grief that has
made a home of my father's eyes. i have spent many nights wishing i
could piece their hearts together again—
but i still haven't quite figured out how to mend
mine.

the universe wept when we were given the chance to love each other
and we tore each other apart instead.

some hate themselves and they want you to hate yourself *too*.
in an attempt to feel less alone;
to have some company in their despair.

THE DIARY OF A MODERN POET.

i tried to drown my grief but i drowned myself instead.

-i am still catching my breath

my drunken arms have danced with the wrong people;
and my drunken lips have spilled my worst secrets.
my drunken mind wanted to destroy me so i decided to
destroy it
first.

i've buried many things in my time.
and the thing is—
they never *stayed* buried.
they'd resurrect, each time quicker than the last.
exhausted from digging, i sat down with them.
and this was when i realized that they'd never go away—
not *completely*.
but, they don't seem so scary now that
i've spent time with them.

the sadness that i experience so often does not belong to me.
well, not to begin with.
i first see it in another's eyes—
then i make it my own.
i'm not sure why i soak up pain the way that i do.
i'm not sure why i can see the dark circles behind their concealer
and i'm not sure why i can hear their sorrows and secrets in their
voice,
but *i do*; and i've never known how to stop.

-empath

most sorrow we feel for a reason.
to teach us; to guide us.
but— there are certain kinds of sorrow that i'm not sure why exist.
sorrow so tragic you can't think of any reason as to why it would.
sorrow; that feels like your soul has been torn from your body
because it just couldn't bear to live there anymore.

i've always felt comforted on rainy days. i love hearing the taps on
my bedroom window.
each tap sounds like the clouds reminding me to let go.
they say
   'see? we're doing it and ***you can too.*** *'*

i'd have given my life to make sure he got to live his.
simply because—
i loved him.
and *love* is something greater than ourselves.

THE DIARY OF A MODERN POET.

the tricky thing about grief is
 you never know when it'll show up
or how.

-unannounced visitor

i could never bear being in the presence of the heavy-hearted. i
always want to take the weight off of them and make it my own.
if i could,
i'd bottle their tears and tell them not to worry;
they're *mine now.*

my brother and i are the same in a lot of ways.
one difference is—
he cannot forgive the people that have hurt him the way that i can
forgive the people that have hurt me.
that's why i've always been a little more *sad*
and he's always been a little more *angry*.

i see so much of myself in my mother

and i know she sees the same in me

like we feel the same kind of sad
and the same kind of happy.
-her blueprint

he loved me in the mornings when i was still too tired to speak;
and he loved me on the nights i spent too intoxicated to *think*.
he only loved me when i was a watered down version of myself;
like a glass of iced tea after the ice cubes had melted and didn't taste
too bitter anymore.

he searched for my flaws; under the bed, in the closet, and in the
pockets of my jeans. and when he finally discovered enough— he
read them off to me as he packed his bags. it was painful;
him not knowing that not wanting to stay was enough reason to leave.
and he didn't have to rip this house to shreds looking for reasons to
feel satisfied by it.

if you allow them,
people who are envious of you will
hack off your wings and tell you that
you look better that way.

your affection had a price.
and no matter how hard i worked,
i somehow *always* came up empty handed.

and when i picture my heart, i picture scotch tape, staples, and an at-home stitch job. i picture a fragile, messy thing that's held together by any and everything i could find. and i never know at what moment it will all start to unravel.

i grew tired of knives in my back;
so i started wearing armor.

THE DIARY OF A MODERN POET.

we died
 a long time ago

but i still visit our burial site
with flowers in one hand
and my poetry in the other

and as i stare at the ground,
i ask myself
what could i have done to save us

the answer is always
nothing

and you're not my garden to water anymore.
but—
i still peek my head over the fence from time to time;
just to see how much you've grown.

i have never understood how someone could fall out of love in an instance. for me, falling out of love feels like i've been walking miles to a destination i'm not sure i'll ever reach before my legs collapse and i tell myself i can't go on any longer;

not like this.

if you pay close enough attention, you'll see that most of us are
zombies;
living— but not really *alive*.

THE DIARY OF A MODERN POET.

you think you're fighting a war together;
for each other.
then suddenly
you realize—
they are the one shooting at you.

losing someone you love is like
cutting off a limb
and still feeling the ache

- ghost pains

THE DIARY OF A MODERN POET.

he told me that i lived my life like it was a movie
and i thought to myself
that he was my favorite scene.

people make a mockery of those who have strayed from reality.
but they never think that maybe there is a reason they're so far gone;
a place so sorrowful
they needed to run away from.

waiting for somebody to come back
is like digging yourself a grave.
you need to *live*,
not lay down in the same place they left you.

i have loved him for as long as i've known him and i will continue to love him long after that.

THE DIARY OF A MODERN POET.

if these four walls could talk, they'd say that they've seen resilience.
they'd say that i have cried so loud, it pierced them—
probably enough for the neighbors to hear. they'd say that i have
turned too many full bottles into empty ones, like it was my favorite
magic trick. and they'd say that i have gotten better. that i smile more.
and that i haven't performed
my favorite magic trick for quite some time. if these four walls could
talk, i'd tell them thank you. i'd tell them that i'll love them
forever— even when i'm not here anymore. and they'd tell me

they love me too

-written from my bedroom

THE DIARY OF A MODERN POET.

i don't think my heart
will ever stop aching

even on it's happiest days
it asks

how could you
how could you
how could you

i felt small with him; insignificant. screaming up from the floor 'i'm here, i'm right here!'

endings for me have always felt explosive;
all at once then calmer over time.
our ending wasn't explosive— it's an aching, a longing;
like my soul had been in love with yours in a previous life
and this time—
she thought she'd get to keep you.

we wept more than we laughed

-why we ended

i made the mistake of loving him with everything i had; so when he left,
i had nothing for myself.

i've sat with monsters long enough
to recognize their friends.

i've never liked to admit that my biggest fear is being alone. and i don't mean that i fear i cannot find someone to spend my life with— i believe that's quite easy. i fear that i'll never find one that lights a fire in me; enough for me to *want* to spend a lifetime with them. and i fear that if i ever do, i am giving them the weapon that can destroy all that i've built.

you focus so much on finding love in other people because it is nowhere to be found in yourself.

i stumbled through life
waiting to run into the thing or the person that would save me. and
someone *did*—
until they left and i felt as afraid as i did before they found me. i
learned that people can only *truly* save themselves.
i learned that waiting to be rescued
will only ever get you killed.

and for the longest time,
the end of a chapter felt like abandonment and
the word goodbye sounded like *betrayal*.

it's strange, the way that sadness
feels sort of warm; like it's someone i used to know very well but
stopped coming around.
and now, when sadness visits me again,
i tell her to make herself at home.

my heart will ask you not to go
while my hand holds the door open for you.

and in the midst of heartbreak,
i am reminded just how lucky i am to ache.
i will not be here forever—
so i will feel all that i can before i have to go.

do not hold onto things out of selfishness.
if you won't wear the sneakers again,
give them to someone *who will.* if you won't love someone with all
that you have, let them go so they can experience it by the hands of
someone else.
people and things deserve to be held by someone who appreciates
them—
just as they are.

instead of shaming the parts of myself that i didn't love, i sat down
with them. i asked them why they were there—
and what they needed.
and suddenly it all made sense.
i realized that they were only so loud because they needed to be seen;
not shamed.

chapter 4

the beginning and the end

i have always gotten lost
in the people that i love.
i used to call it loyalty; now i call it betrayal.

-i belong to me first

there was a point in time where i only knew to write about pain. my pen was useless without a half-empty bottle on my nightstand and tears rolling off my chin magically turning into ink. i'm glad i found more joy in this life and have learned to write from it;
for there is beauty in pain but
there's beauty in hope *too*.

forgive me
for the times i picked your petals apart
playing
do you love
do you love me not

instead of just allowing them to grow

i wish i knew better then, but i didn't.
i suppose that's the whole point, after all.
pain teaches us;
like a child who touches a hot stove.

and in that moment, i was reminded that some things truly cannot be fixed; that the glue can come apart at any minute and you're stuck cleaning up the mess again.
some things are just broken forever.
and *that's okay.*

it'd be easy to say he never loved me. but *he did.*
he just didn't love me the way i needed to be loved.
i required more than he was equipped to give and that's *okay.*
he just needs someone who is *less.*
and i need someone who is *more.*
our love taught me that **incompatibility**
doesn't always have to end in flames.
incompatibility can end in a warm goodbye;
a 'i hope you find someone who knows how to love you better than i
can.'

we were meant to love each other
but we weren't meant to be *in love*

-parting ways with your best friend

you don't know how to not feel everything all at once,
and that's why you're hurting more
but it's also why you'll heal *faster*.

our love still exists. and maybe it's not in the same bed anymore; or even the same city. but it exists— in the photo of us that i know you still keep in your wallet. in the post-it note with 'i love you' written on it still in my nightstand. our love still dances in the kitchen and our laughter still echoes throughout this house. our love still exists— it's just different now. it's a memory, a photo, a post-it note; a ghost.

the world will keep spinning
with or without you

it's up to you to choose
how long you stand still;
how much you *miss*.

i fear that i've gotten obsessed with the idea of healing, of getting
better, of fixing myself.
like i'm this never-ending project that i'm too scared to
reveal until i am perfected.
i must remember that i can show up while still being a work in
progress; that i can't hide myself until i am perfect—
because then i would have spent my whole life hiding.

you reached out to me
years later

curiosity masquerading as an apology
to see if i'm still within your grasp

i'm not

time will sneak up on you.
sometimes in the loveliest of ways.
one day you'll be driving down the highway,
feeling the warmth of the golden sunset on your arms and humming
along to the radio.
you'll think to yourself in this moment 'i'm so *happy*.'
and this surprises you because it feels like only yesterday your heart
was broken into a million pieces.
ah, time— <u>what a very sneaky thing it is.</u>

and for the longest time, i couldn't see without
someone else's lantern
guiding me through the dark.
after time,
i've *become* the lantern.

THE DIARY OF A MODERN POET.

if i died today,
i would be satisfied.
i spent my days falling in love with the mundane moments.
the feeling of warm water on my skin,
the mornings of waking up to the smell of cooking,
the sound of rain hitting the roof of the house,
the late nights spent drunk and dancing with
someone you love in the kitchen.
if i died today,
i could go confidently knowing that i loved life;
that i paid attention to the things that are most overlooked.
that when i laughed, i laughed until my stomach ached.
when i cried, i cried until i could cry no longer.
and when i loved,
i loved with every cell of this body.

THE DIARY OF A MODERN POET.

writing poetry
is like ripping my chest apart
and letting the tsunamis of hurt
pour out onto paper.

my arms grew tired from reaching out to yours—
making sure that we crossed that bridge together. so i crossed it
alone.

-then i watched it fall apart

i hope that i am remembered not for who i've been
but for who i've become.
i want to be remembered for loving deeply,
for being a little strange, for writing passionately,
and for always finding beauty in the mundane.
i want someone to look out the window as it rains a little too hard
and think
'she would've loved this.'

i wept when i lost you;
and now i shed tears of joy,
because how lucky was i—
to have to loved someone *that* much;
to have such a difficult goodbye.

nostalgia is your worst enemy.
it seems to erase
all the pain on memory lane and
shines a spotlight on the good
sprinkled in here and there

it says
'you miss this.'

but i promise,

you don't.

do not trust every 'i love you' spoken.
anyone could utter those three special words;
sometimes, 'i love you' means:

i love your body.
i love what you can offer me.
i love the way that
you
love
me.

and here's to love.
the love that stayed and the love that left.
the love that broke us and the love that delicately glued our pieces
together.
the love that we pour into the world without ever asking for it back
and the love that we give to ourselves— on our good days

and *especially,* our bad.

it's okay to sit and lick
your wounds for awhile—
but do not fail to see
when it's time to start living again.

i was always made for more than *you.*
and that's why as hard as i tried,
the universe grabbed me by my hand and reminded me that i could
not be yours—
and you could not be mine.

contrary to what you might believe,
the ability to forgive does not make you weak.
the ability to forgive is a skill that most spend their *whole lives*
mastering—
so if it comes naturally to you,
cherish it.

i've spent too long repairing my little world to
let just anyone in here with me.
they must be gentle enough to not destroy what i've built;
and they must be loving enough to never want to.

i know one thing to be true:
i sprinkle a little bit of magic everywhere i go.
a little bit of love.
a little bit of warmth.

i was utterly frightened of the space that you left behind.
a room once filled with love now filled with
cobwebs and empty boxes.
i sat on the floor for months,
with a bottle in my hand,
afraid to look at where you once sat next to me.
then one sunday morning, hungover, i brought myself to look at your
old spot and i realized;
this place didn't *have* to be so empty. i began to hang art on the walls,
piled poetry books onto the shelves, and stocked up on warm
blankets. i lit candles and i started playing my favorite music again.
this place *was* scary at one point in time, but now, it's as beautiful as
it's ever been. *so* beautiful that—

i'm glad you left it behind.

i love surrounding myself with the feelers,
the thinkers, the lovers, and the dreamers;
where we are all a little strange,
but strange doesn't phase us—
because we have all been alive long enough
to know that strange really just means interesting.

i strive to be warm;
so warm, that it wraps around the people i love like a blanket.
hell, i want acquaintances and strangers to feel it too.
i want to shout to the world that they're safe with me;
that when winter seems to be overstaying it's visit,
there's a place for them here,
where it's always spring.

i've found that the more something is exaggerated—
the less likely it is to be true.
when someone says *'i'm happy'*, i believe them.
but if they scream it from the rooftops and
wear it on their shirts,
i can't help but think that they're not only trying to convince others,
but that they're desperately trying to
convince themselves too.

one day it just happened

i stopped writing
i stopped calling

the 'i miss you's'
that were once meant for them
became for me

the old me might as well have stood out on the street with a sign that read "love me, love me, love me". she so desperately wanted to be loved—

so i gave it to her.

you asked me where i buried her
i said:
somewhere far away

-when they tell you 'you've changed'

i wish i could say that i have never abandoned myself—
but it wouldn't be true. i ran so far from
myself that it took what seemed like forever
to find my way back.

THE DIARY OF A MODERN POET.

if it is true that our homes represent our minds:
then my mind is the color orange—
it's filled with photos of the people that i care for.
it is a fixer-upper. there are some parts that i probably should have
worked on by now but *i'll get there.*
it gets messy sometimes—
dirty clothes sprawled out on the staircase and leftovers that i have
yet to put away. but,
nothing a little determination cannot fix.
it can get lonely as it's only me here,
but lonely isn't always a bad thing.
because it is quiet and if it ever gets *too* quiet, i can sing as loud as i
want to.
so, if it is true that our homes represent our minds:
then i am happy to call this my home.

THE DIARY OF A MODERN POET.

i used to think that i didn't have anyone
until i crawled out of the hole that i had dug
for myself and heard cheering

-i was loved all along

there are few people who have seen me for what i am
and did not run. for most of my life, i feared i was too much;
too strange to love.
i started camouflaging myself to look just like everyone else,
saying
'look, i'm just like you!'
even today, my abnormalities feel like a burden.
but i have spent many years trying to blend in and
i could never shake the feeling that blending in was really just
self-abandonment.
which i could not do any longer, because even *if* no one else could
love me,
wouldn't not loving myself be
so much worse?

i'm not sure if i will fall in love again.
at least,
not with anyone else.
for now,
i'm just learning how to love myself.

i choose to be celebrated;
not tolerated.
i'd sit in solitude before i place myself in a room
where i am not entirely wanted ever again.

there are parts of you that are just *for you.*
you don't owe the entirety of who you are to
other people. it's okay to preserve just a
few little pieces.

THE DIARY OF A MODERN POET.

our branches have grown in opposite directions;
to the point where i don't think we'll ever touch again.
but i find comfort in knowing that our roots are so deeply intertwined
that you'll always be a part of me— and i, you.
and even though we grew apart,
we once grew *together*.

you *think* that there's no one out there like you until someone falls in
love with your art;
or you fall in love with someone else's and
you realize that you're not quite as alone as
you thought you were.

i have grown to love something i was once deathly afraid of;
my solitude.

i want a love that consumes me entirely;
a love that never dreams of walking away.
i want passion and adoration.
anything less is mediocre and while many things in this life are
allowed to be mediocre,
love **is not one of them.**

i hope love finds me again.
and when it does,
i hope i'm ready for it.

i am grateful that i learned how to quiet my tides.
i let them overpower me for so long—
they'd destroy the cities that i had worked hard to build and
sometimes hurt the people that resided in them.
it took decades of chaos to learn to be calm.
and i am still myself;
perhaps *more* myself than ever.

i searched tirelessly for other people's warmth because i thought that i
didn't have any of my own.
then i shut the door i left open for the people who walked in and out
of my life;
and lit a match to the fireplace in my chest that had collected dust all
these years.
i think to myself 'ah, *there it is.* '

i am learning to care for myself the way i'd care for a dear friend. **and this is the beginning and the end of everything.**

www.ingramcontent.com/pod-product-compliance
Lightning Source LLC
Chambersburg PA
CBHW071217090426
42736CB00014B/2866